# CRAWL, BITE & STING! DEADLY INSECTS
# INSECTS FOR KIDS ENCYCLOPEDIA

## Children's Bug & Spider Books

**BABY PROFESSOR**
EDUCATION KIDS

Speedy Publishing LLC
40 E. Main St. #1156
Newark, DE 19711
www.speedypublishing.com
Copyright 2017

In this book, we're going to talk about some of the deadliest insects and spiders on Earth. So, let's get right to it!

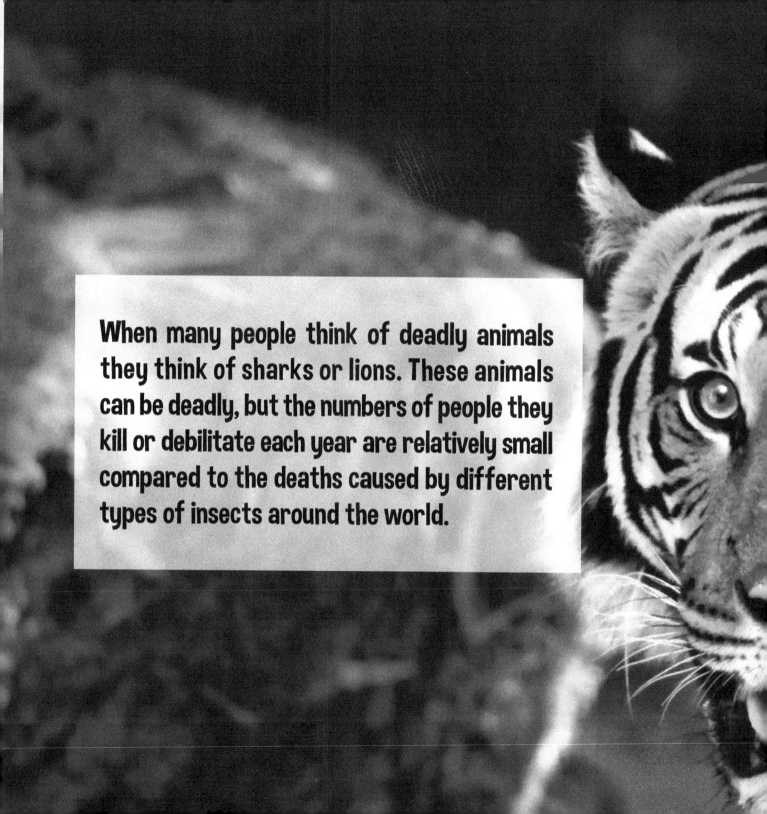

When many people think of deadly animals they think of sharks or lions. These animals can be deadly, but the numbers of people they kill or debilitate each year are relatively small compared to the deaths caused by different types of insects around the world.

BLACK WIDOW SPIDER

The bites and stings from insects and spiders don't usually kill right away. One of the ways that these creatures kill people is that they transmit deadly diseases that are caused by the microscopic creatures they carry in their bodies.

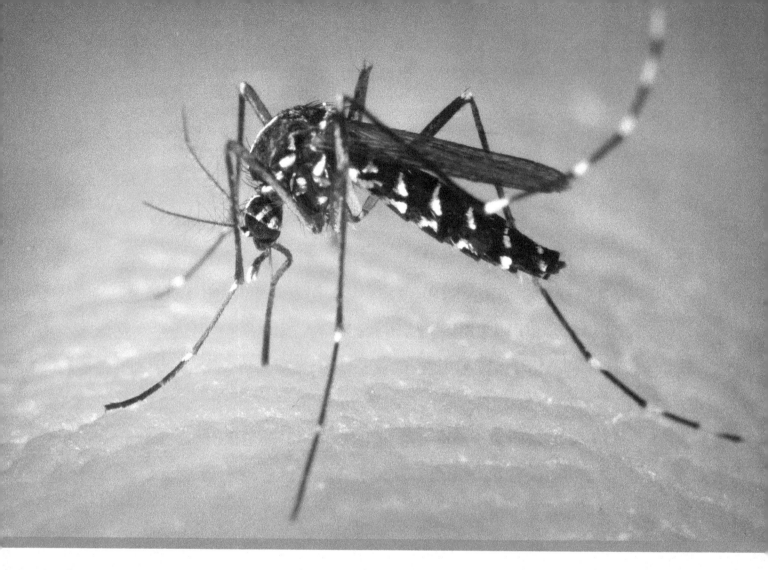

Sharks kill about 10 people annually and lions kill about 100 every year. Mosquitoes, the deadliest of all insects, carry a host of painful and sometimes lethal diseases and are responsible for killing over 725,000 people every year.

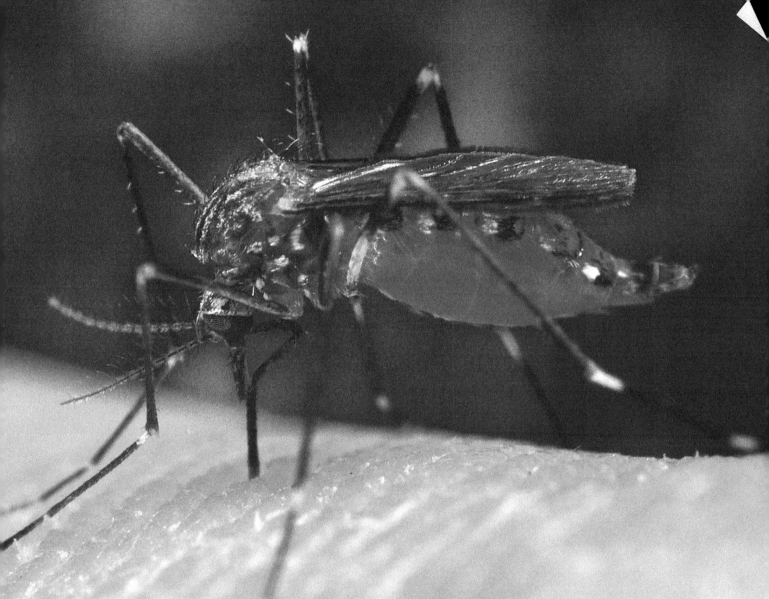

Some insects can inject deadly toxins into our veins or bury their eggs under our skin.

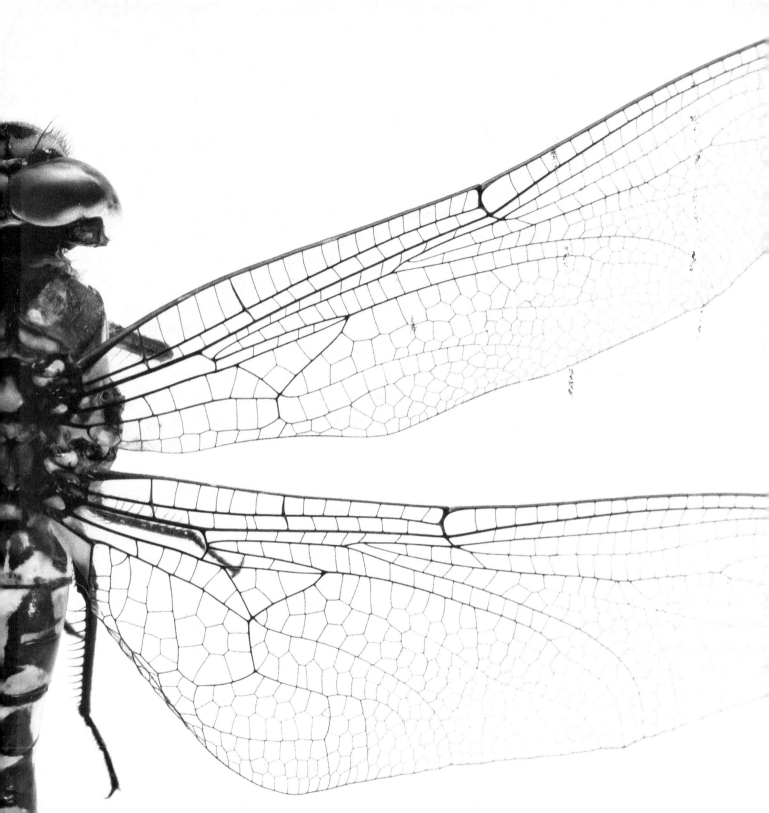

Here are some of the deadliest insects on Earth and the ways that they cause destruction to their prey and to people.

# THE AFRICAN ASSASSIN BUG

The venom of the African assassin bug is ten times as toxic as cobra snake venom. Luckily, this black and yellow bug doesn't produce as much venom as a cobra produces. Native to Africa as its name suggests, the African assassin bug releases its venom either by spitting it at its attacker or potential prey or by injecting it.

AFRICAN ASSASSIN BUG

When the African assassin bug attacks another insect it wants to eat, it injects it with its venom, which liquefies the organs of its prey. Then, the assassin bug places its proboscis into the insect it killed and drinks its prey's liquefied remains. If you are bitten by an assassin bug, you won't necessarily die, but more than one bite could cause you considerable pain. Despite the danger, some people have African assassin bugs as pets!

# AFRICANIZED HONEYBEES

In the year 1956, a scientist in Brazil named Warwick Kerr imported some honeybees from Africa to his laboratory in South America. Some of the African honeybees escaped and mated with European honeybees creating a new hybrid species.

AFRICANIZED HONEYBEES

The populations of these Africanized honeybees, nicknamed "killer bees," began to increase and eventually they could be found across South and Central America into Mexico, California, and the southwest region of the United States.

The Africanized honeybee is actually a little smaller than the European honeybee so its sting emits less venom.

However, the reason that the Africanized honeybees are much more dangerous is due to the way they swarm.

If an animal or person threatens their hive, they go into a fury and attack viciously. Over the last five decades hundreds of people have been killed when thousands of bees swarmed. Some people are highly allergic to bee stings, but in general it takes about 1,000 stings to kill a person. Africanized honeybees have been known to chase their attacker for more than half a mile before giving up the chase.

# THE HUMAN BOT FLY

Bot flies primarily live in Central America as well as South America, but they can be found worldwide. Different species of the bot fly target different kinds of animals as well as specific parts of their bodies, such as the sheep nose bot fly.

Unfortunately, there is a human bot fly as well. The human bot fly finds warm, wet areas of human tissue for a location to mate and lay their eggs.

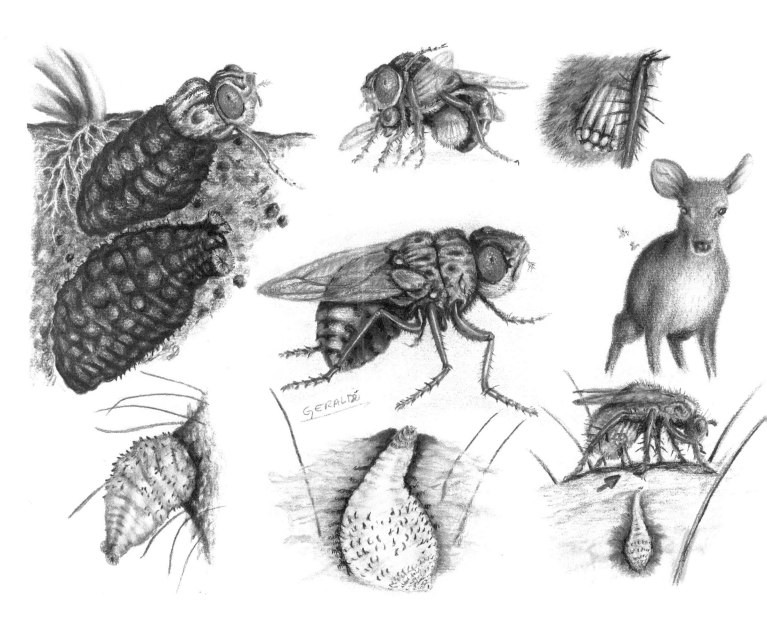

GERALDO

HUMAN BOTFLY LIFE CYCLE

Then, their hatched larvae dig down into the skin and consume the human tissue. Any warm, moist tissue will serve their purposes including the tissue of the brain!

# THE BRAZILIAN WANDERING SPIDER

**T**he spider with the most powerful venom worldwide is called the Brazilian wandering spider. Spiders aren't insects. Instead, they are arachnids along with scorpions, ticks, and mites. Native to the jungles of Brazil, this scary spider has a type of venom composed of a neurotoxin that's similar in composition to another venomous spider, the black widow spider.

BRAZILIAN WANDERING SPIDER

One bite immediately yields intense pain, cold sweats, and a heart beat that's irregular.

If the bite isn't treated, the victim dies or experiences horribly painful symptoms.

# THE BULLET ANT

**T**he bullet ant lives in the rainforests from Nicaragua in Central America to Paraguay in South America. The reason it's called a bullet ant is because if this 1-inch-long ant bites you it feels like you have an incredibly painful bullet wound.

BULLET ANT

It's been ranked as the most painful bite of any known insect. As if this wasn't bad enough, these ants live on and around trees and they will let out a shrieking sound before they bite you to warn you to stay away from their tree nests.

One bite may not kill you but will give you horrible spasms for a long time afterwards and if you receive multiple bites it could be fatal.

# THE JAPANESE HORNET

**M**ore than 70 people are killed each year by Japanese hornets. This huge 3-inch-long insect has a very painful sting, which is considered to be the most painful insect sting of any flying insect. The venom it injects into its victim is composed of eight toxins of different types.

**JAPANESE HORNET**

As soon as the toxin gets into a person's body it begins to destroy tissue and to make matters even worse, the hornet releases a pheromone, which is a scent that makes other hornets attracted to the location of the sting.

# MOSQUITOES

It's common to get a mosquito bite when you're outdoors for any length of time in the evening. Mosquitoes are small midgelike flies that suck blood. The itching and redness people experience after getting bitten by a mosquito is a reaction to the mosquito's saliva. Fortunately, most mosquitoes don't carry diseases that are harmful to humans.

There are 3,000 different species, but only three types are lethal to humans and these transmit diseases from microorganisms and viruses they carry.

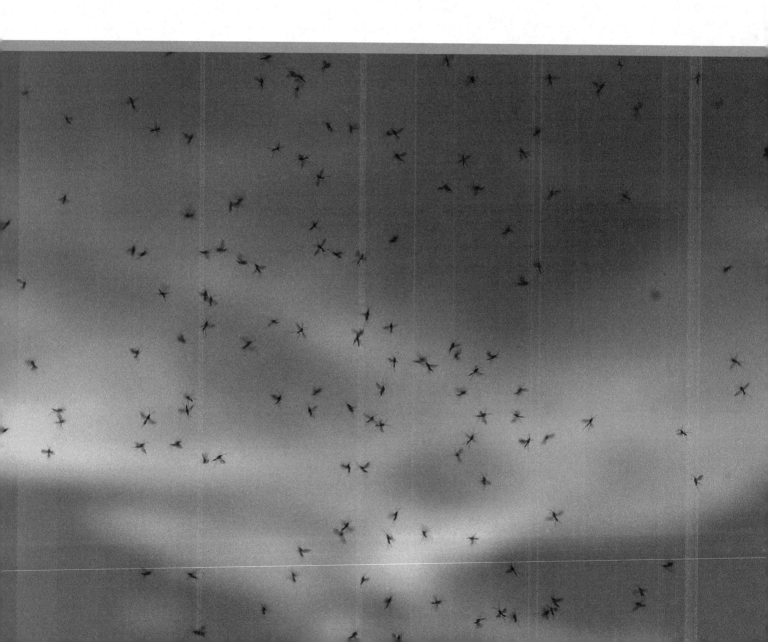

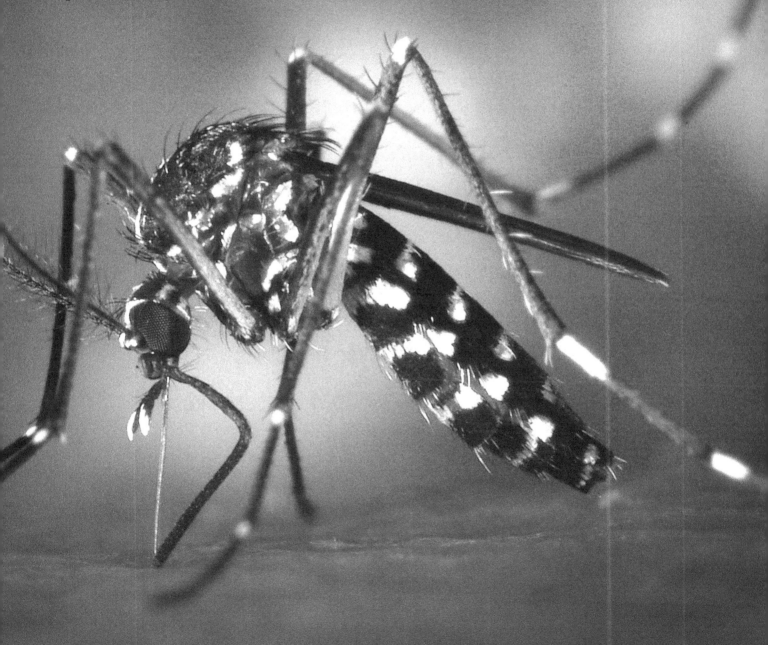

However, the disease-carrying types cause thousands and perhaps millions of deaths around the world each year.

They carry many different types of diseases, such as:

- Dengue Fever, a disease that causes high fever and joint pain

- West Nile Virus, a disease that damages the circulatory system and brain tissue

- Malaria, a disease that destroys liver function and then causes severe fever and chills

- Yellow Fever, a disease that causes severe headache, nausea, and fever

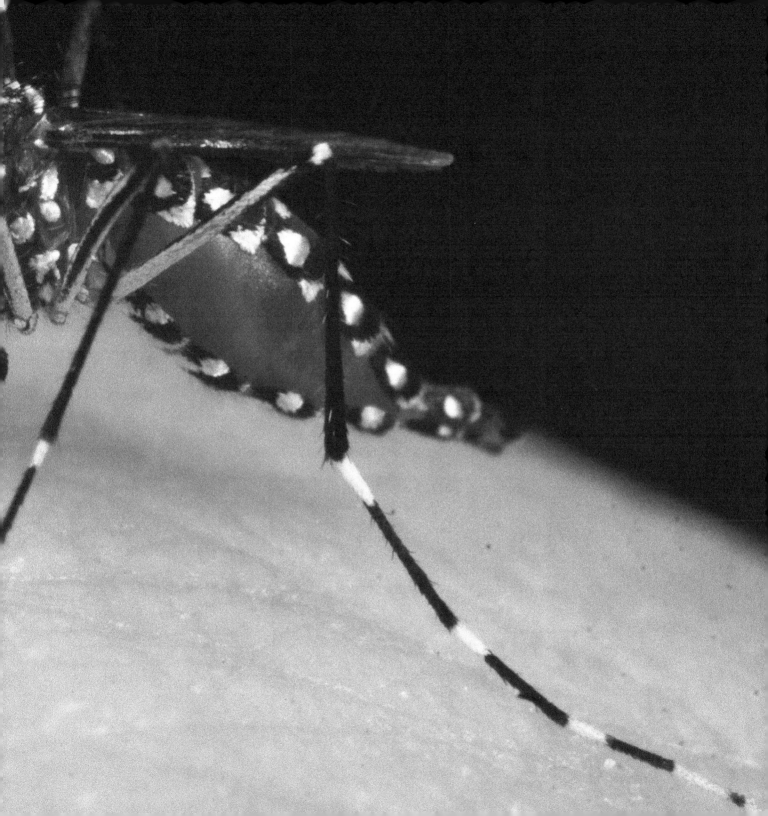

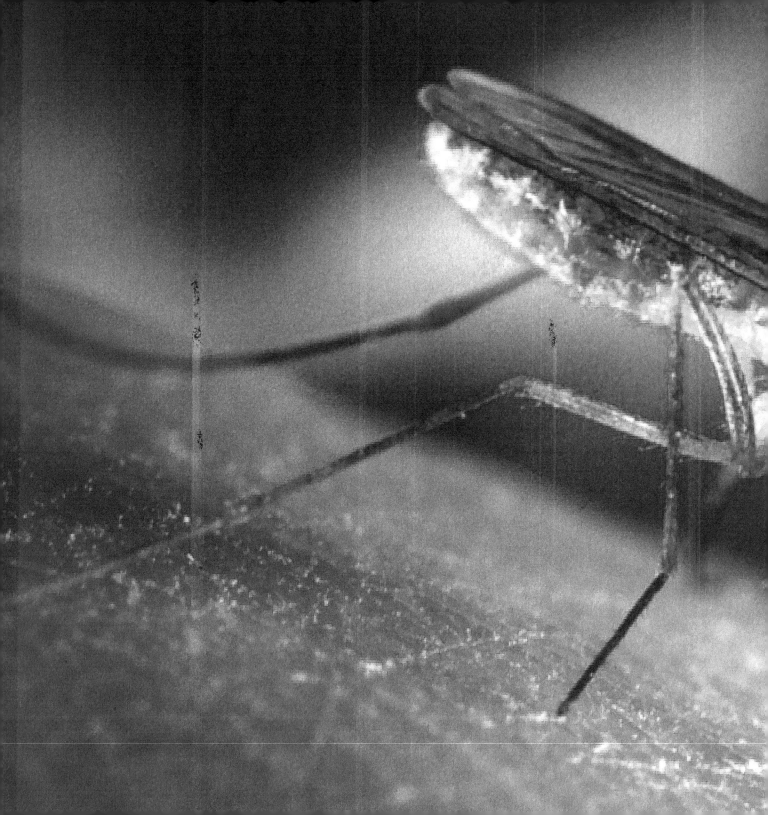

- Murray Valley Encephalitis, a disease that causes damage to brain tissue, headaches, and seizures

- Chikungunya, a disease that causes headache, vomiting, and rashes on the skin

- Japanese Encephalitis, a disease that causes headaches, convulsions, and coma

In many areas of the world, mosquitoes are a major threat to people.

# SIAFU ANTS OR AFRICAN ANTS

**S**iafu ants or African ants live in enormous colonies in the central and eastern part of Africa. A single bite might not do much harm, but these deadly ants live in enormous colonies with populations of twenty million or more ants.

ARMY ANTS

They go on marches where they devour everything in their path. For their size, they have large jaws like scissors. They dice up their prey and spread a dissolving acid on it so it liquefies.

They eat on the run. The only defense you have is to get out of their way. Some insects stay perfectly still and avoid being bitten, because the army ants detect their prey by movement.

# THE TSETSE FLY

**F**ound in the countries of Central Africa, the tsetse fly is about the same size as an ordinary housefly. Tsetse flies carry a lethal protozoa described as Trypanosomes. These microorganisms cause an illness called Sleeping Sickness, which attacks a person's central nervous system.

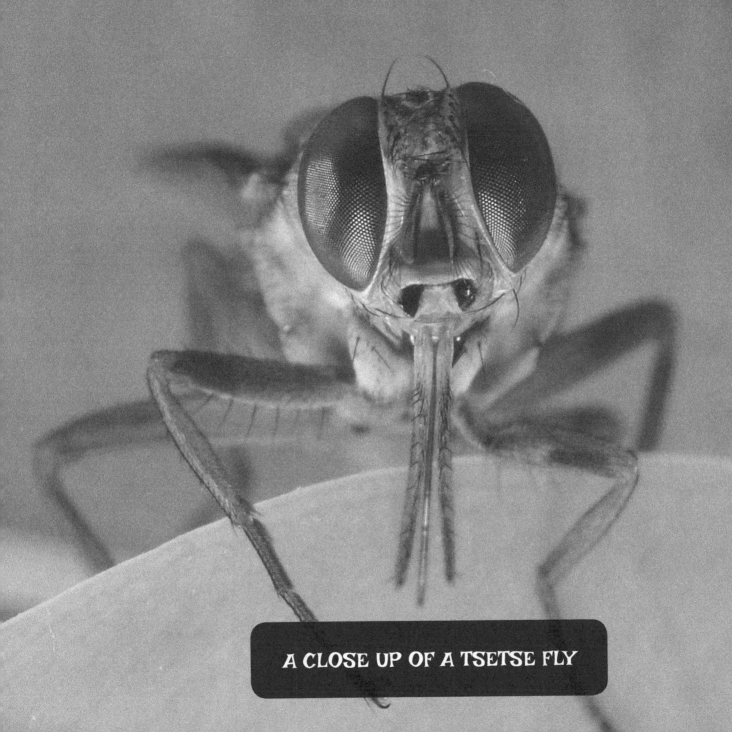

A CLOSE UP OF A TSETSE FLY

It causes the person to have changes in his or her ability to coordinate and sleep. If left untreated, the person can die. There are no vaccines available to ensure a person isn't susceptible to it. Scientists have discovered that wearing clothing in light colors helps to keep them away since they are attracted to bright colors, especially dark blue.

# HOW TO AVOID DANGEROUS INSECTS

You can avoid some types of dangerous insects by not traveling to tropical regions of the world. However, some lethal insects, especially mosquitoes and some types of spiders, could be lurking in your neighborhood or even your own backyard. Mosquitoes breed in wet areas so make sure to stay away from infested ponds and waterways. When you're going outdoors for a picnic or hike, spray on mosquito repellant and if you're camping make sure to sleep under a mosquito net for protection.

A MOTHER APPLYING INSECT REPELLENT TO HER CHILD

# SMALL BUT TERRIBLE INSECTS

When people think of dangerous animals, they often think of something powerful with large jaws. Ironically, some of the most dangerous animals on Earth are insects. In fact, the common mosquito is the most lethal of all insects since certain species carry deadly diseases. More than 725,000 people each year die from diseases they received through mosquito bites.

**N**ow that you've read about deadly insects you may want to read about birds of prey in the Baby Professor book Swoop, Attack and Kill - Deadly Birds.

CPSIA information can be obtained
at www.ICGtesting.com
Printed in the USA
BVHW010232310820
587669BV00012B/254

9 781541 917163